Deleted

What happens when you
LOOK?

WHAT HAPPENS WHEN ... ?

What Happens When You Breathe?
What Happens When You Catch a Cold?
What Happens When You Eat?
What Happens When You Grow?
What Happens When You Hurt Yourself?
What Happens When You Listen?
What Happens When You Look?
What Happens When You Run?
What Happens When You Sleep?
What Happens When You Talk?
What Happens When You Think?
What Happens When You Touch and Feel?

Library of Congress Cataloging-in-Publication Data

Richardson, Joy.
  What happens when you look?

  (What happens when — ?)
  Bibliography: p.
  Includes index.
  Summary: Describes what happens when our eyes look at objects and
send visual messages to the brain.
  1. Science—Juvenile literature. 2. Science—Experiments—Juvenile
literature. [1. Eye. 2. Vision] I. Maclean, Colin, 1930-   ill. II.
Maclean, Moria, ill. III. Title. IV. Series: Richardson, Joy. What
happens when — ?
Q163.R49 1986   612'.84   86-3677

ISBN 1-55532-134-8
ISBN 1-55532-109-7 (lib. bdg.)

This North American edition first published in 1986 by
Gareth Stevens, Inc.
7317 West Green Tree Road   Milwaukee, Wisconsin 53223, USA

U.S. edition, this format, copyright ©1986
Supplementary text and illustrations copyright ©1986
by Gareth Stevens, Inc.
Illustrations copyright ©1985 by Colin and Moira Maclean

First published in the United Kingdom by Hamish Hamilton Children's
Books with an original text copyright by Joy Richardson.

Typeset by Ries Graphics, ltd.
Series editor: MaryLee Knowlton
Cover design: Gary Moseley
Additional illustration/design: Laurie Shock

What happens when you
LOOK?

Joy Richardson

pictures by
Colin and Moira Maclean

introduction by
Gail Zander, Ph.D.

Gareth Stevens Publishing
Milwaukee

... a note to parents and teachers

Curiosity about the body begins shortly after birth when babies explore with their mouths. Gradually children add to their knowledge through sight, sound, and touch. They ask questions. However, as they grow, confusion or shyness may keep them from asking questions, and they may acquire little knowledge about what lies beneath their skin. More than that, they may develop bad feelings about themselves based on ignorance or misinformation.

The *What Happens When ... ?* series helps children learn about themselves in a way that promotes healthy attitudes about their bodies and how they work. They learn that their bodies are systems of parts that work together to help them grow, stay well, and function. Each book in the series explains and illustrates how one of the systems works.

With the understanding of how their bodies work, children learn the importance of good health habits. They learn to respect the wonders of the body. With knowledge and acceptance of their bodies' parts, locations, and functions, they can develop a healthy sense of self.

This attractive series of books is an invaluable source of information for children who want to learn clear, correct, and interesting facts about how their bodies work.

GAIL ZANDER, Ph.D.
CHILD PSYCHOLOGIST
MILWAUKEE PUBLIC SCHOOLS

Your eyes are small, but
they have a big job to do.

They let in the light
from everything you look at.
They make pictures and
send them to your brain.

Stand by the door.
Look at a chair on the
other side of the room.
Now close your eyes and
walk across the room
to sit on the chair.

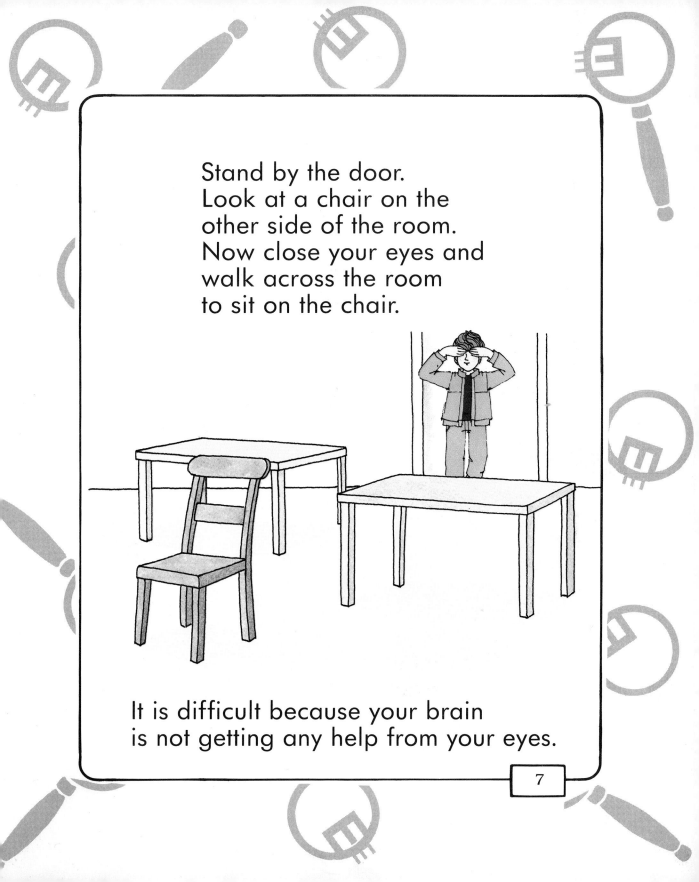

It is difficult because your brain
is not getting any help from your eyes.

Your eyes are like squashy marbles
filled with jelly.
They need protecting.

Close your eyes.
Press a book gently
against one side of your face.

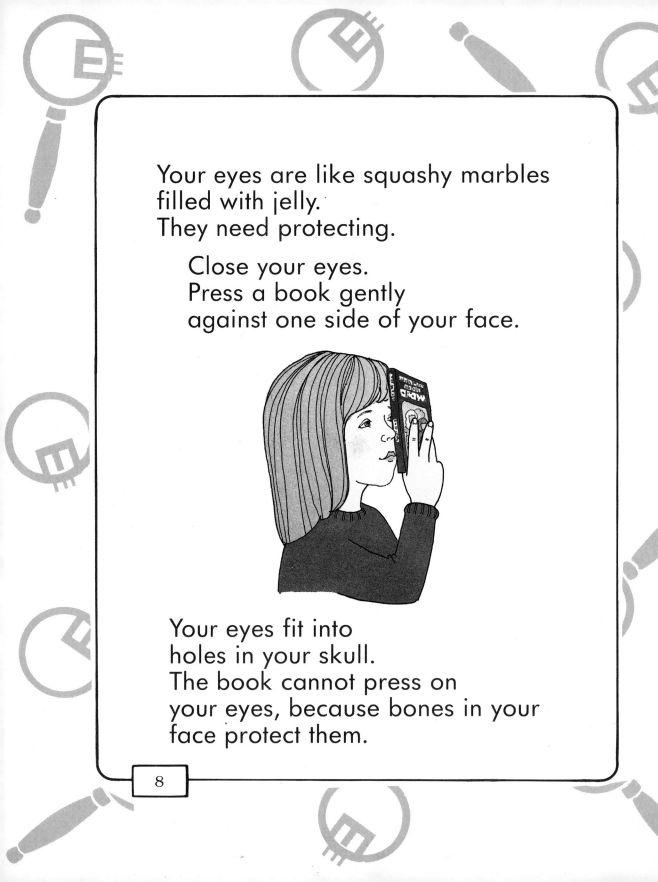

Your eyes fit into
holes in your skull.
The book cannot press on
your eyes, because bones in your
face protect them.

If anything comes too close
to your eyes, you blink.
Your eyelids shut quickly
to keep your eyes safe.

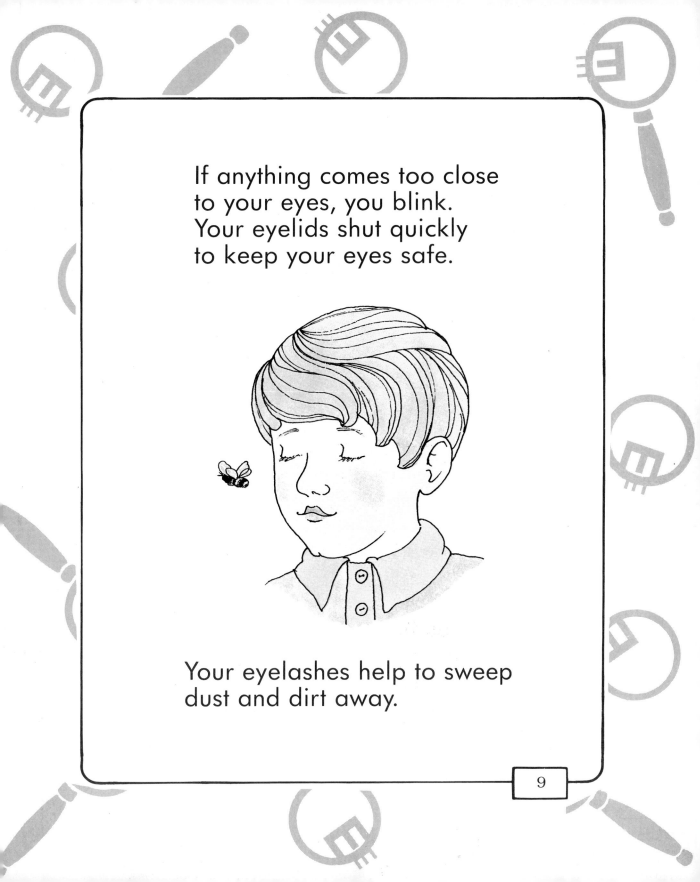

Your eyelashes help to sweep
dust and dirt away.

Tears are made on the
side of your eyeball.
They wash down the front of your eye
and keep it clean and wet.

When you blink, your eyelids
spread tears over your eyes.
You blink about ten times a minute.

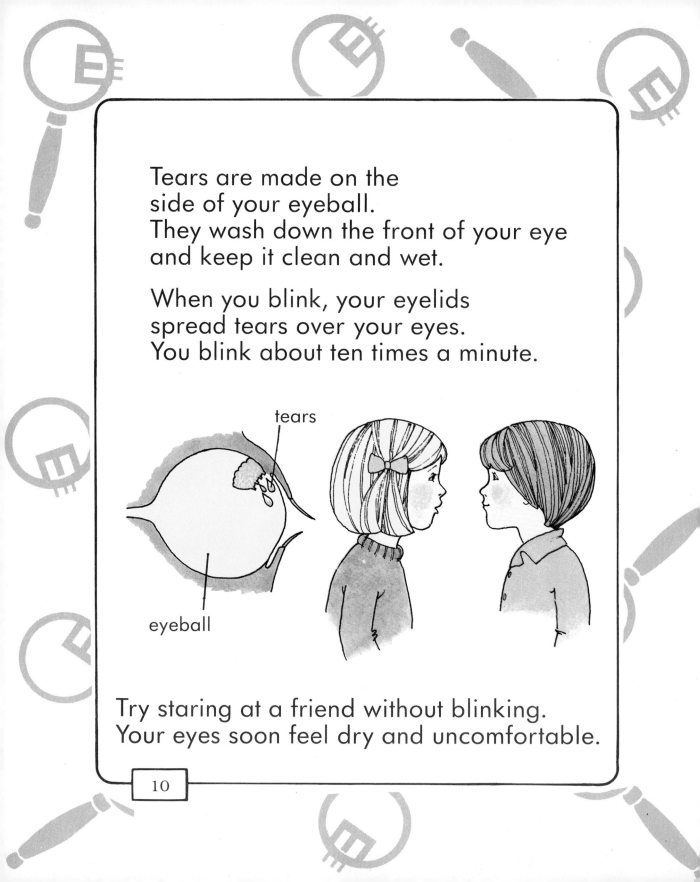

tears

eyeball

Try staring at a friend without blinking.
Your eyes soon feel dry and uncomfortable.

There are tiny holes
in the corners of your eyes.
The tears drain away into your nose.

When you cry, your nose runs.
The extra tears spill down your face.

Animals like rabbits have
eyes on the sides of their heads.
They can see all around and
watch out for enemies.

Your eyes are in front.
You can move them from side to side,
but you cannot see all around.

How far around can you see?

Sit on the floor with your eyes closed.
Ask a friend to collect twelve small things
(like a spoon, a button, a cup, and so on),
and space them evenly around you
in a circle on the floor.

Now open your eyes,
but keep your head still.
Name the things you can see.
How many are out of sight?

In the middle of each eye,
there is a small black hole
covered by clear skin.
It is called your pupil.

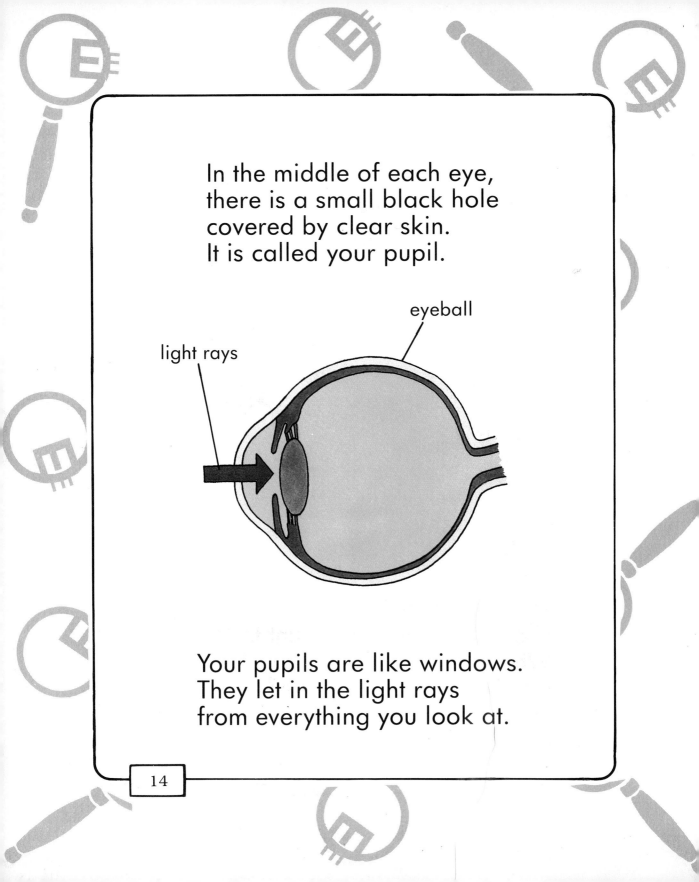

eyeball

light rays

Your pupils are like windows.
They let in the light rays
from everything you look at.

If it is quite dark, your pupils
get bigger to collect more light.
If it is very bright, your pupils
get smaller to let less light in.

Hold a mirror in front of one eye.
Close your eye and count to ten.
What happens to your pupil
when you open your eye?
What happens when you turn toward
the window, and then away again?

Around each pupil you have
a ring of muscles called your iris.
The muscles in your iris
make your pupil bigger or smaller.

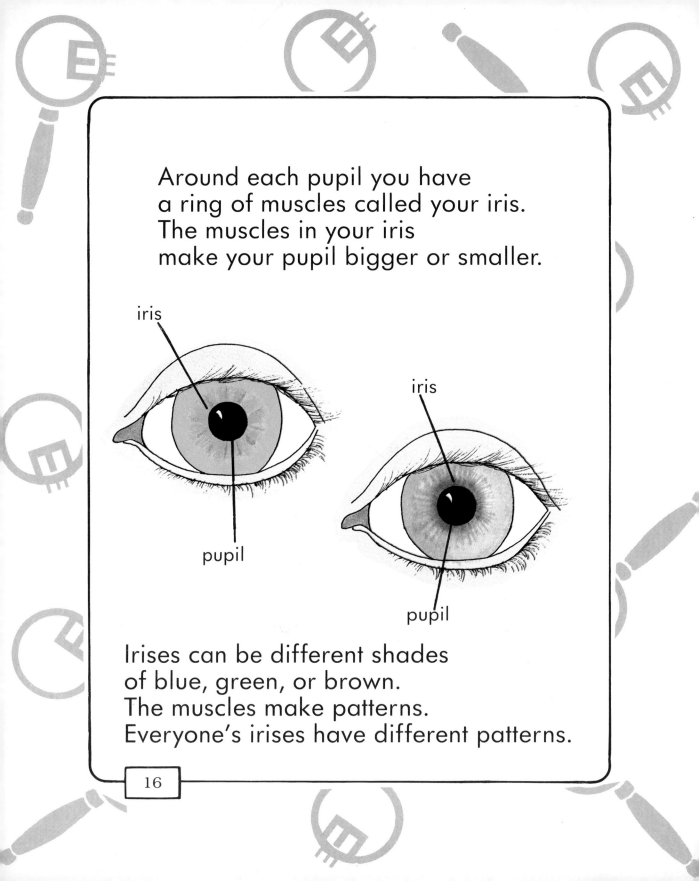

iris

iris

pupil

pupil

Irises can be different shades
of blue, green, or brown.
The muscles make patterns.
Everyone's irises have different patterns.

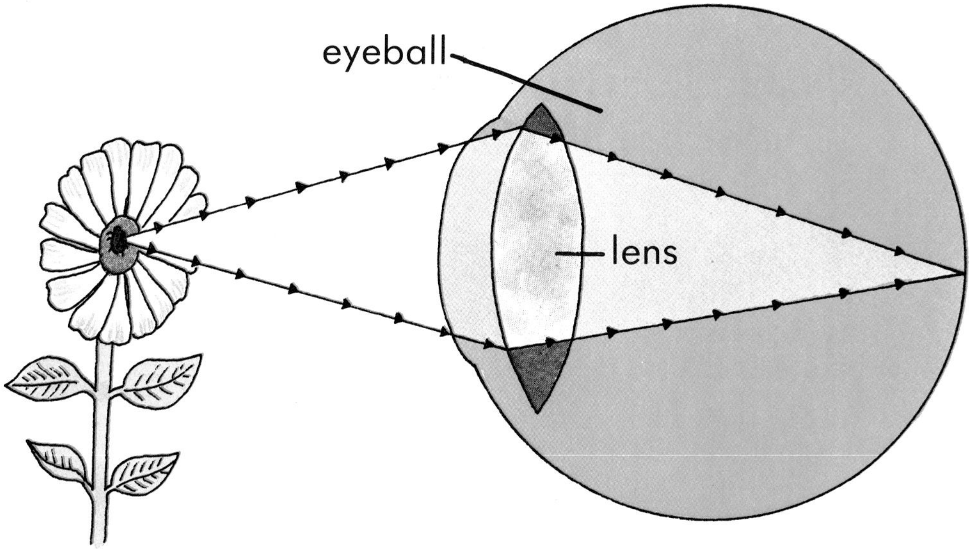

eyeball

lens

Behind each pupil there is
a small round shape called a lens.
The light rays shine through the lens.
The lens bends the light rays
so that they will fit onto a special screen
at the back of your eye.

Look at your finger
through a magnifying glass.
Move the magnifying glass up
and down.

Light rays from your finger come
through the lens in the magnifying glass.
Your finger looks bigger because
the lens bends the light rays
and spreads them out.
If the light rays get too spread out,
your finger looks blurred.

The lens in your eye
can get fatter or thinner
to make clear pictures
of near or faraway things.

Some people wear glasses
because things look blurred.
The lenses in their eyes
are not working properly.
The lenses in their glasses
help to bend the light rays
the right amount.

Hold this book very close to your face.
Look at a word on the first line.
Now look just over the top of the book
at something on the wall.

When you focus on the word,
the wall looks blurred.
When you focus on the wall,
the word looks blurred.

Your eyes can see a lot at once,
but they can only focus clearly
on one thing at a time.

Your eyes zoom in closer together
to look at near things.
They move further apart to
look at faraway things.

Hold up a small toy.
Ask your friend to keep looking at it.
Move it closer and closer to her eyes
and then further and further away.
Watch her eyes moving.

Light rays make a picture on the
screen at the back of your eye.
The thing you are focusing on
is right in the middle.

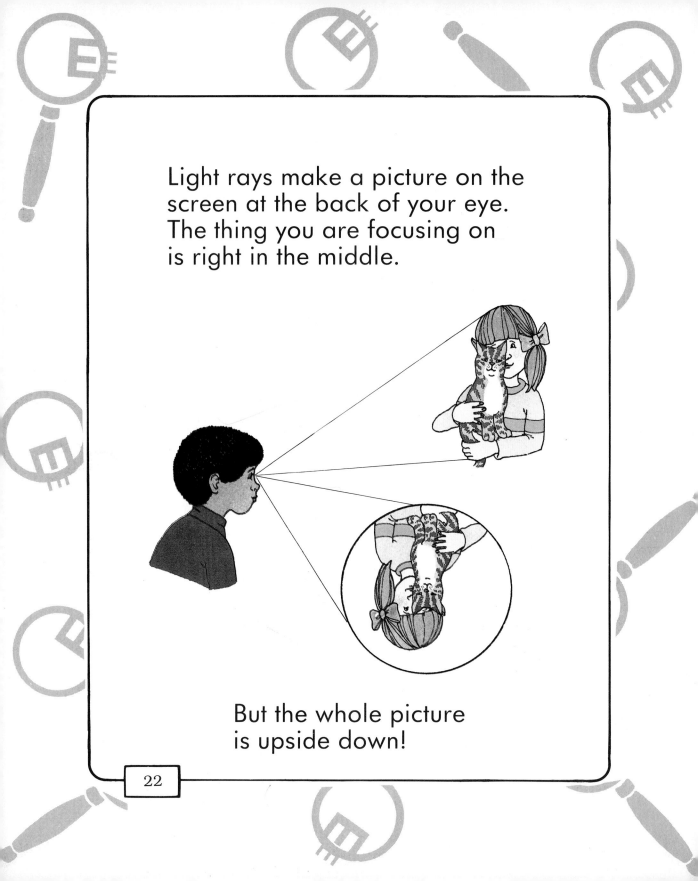

But the whole picture
is upside down!

(1) Draw an eye on a matchbox cover. Make a hole for the pupil.

(2) Cut a tree as tall as this page out of stiff paper. Push colored plastic straws through holes at the top and bottom of the tree.

(3) Push the other ends through the pupil hole to the back of the matchbox.

(4) The straws are like light rays. They have to cross over to get through the small pupil hole. So the picture appears upside down.

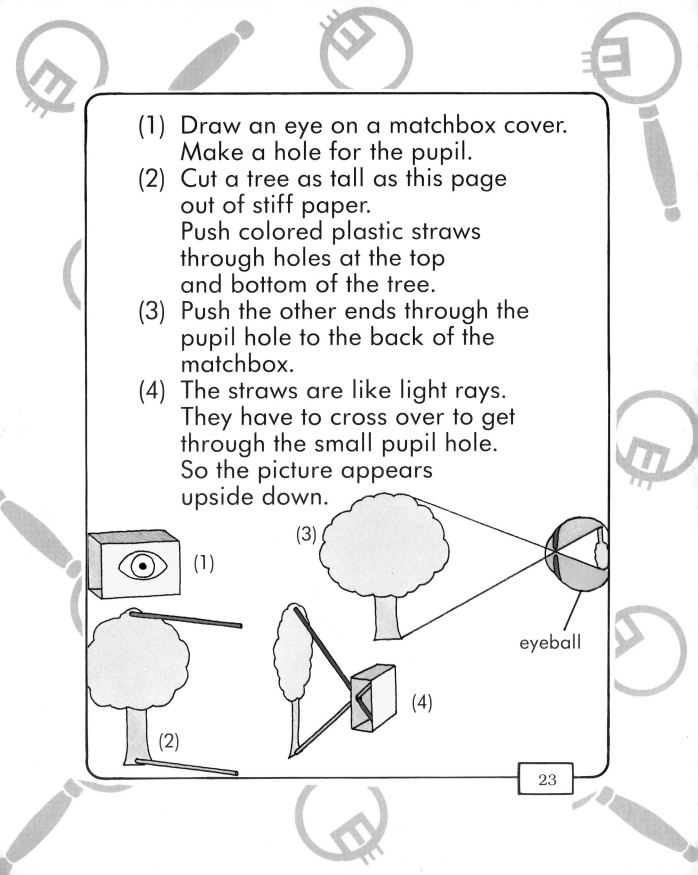

(1)

(2)

(3)

(4)

eyeball

The screen at the back of your eye
is made of millions of tiny cells.

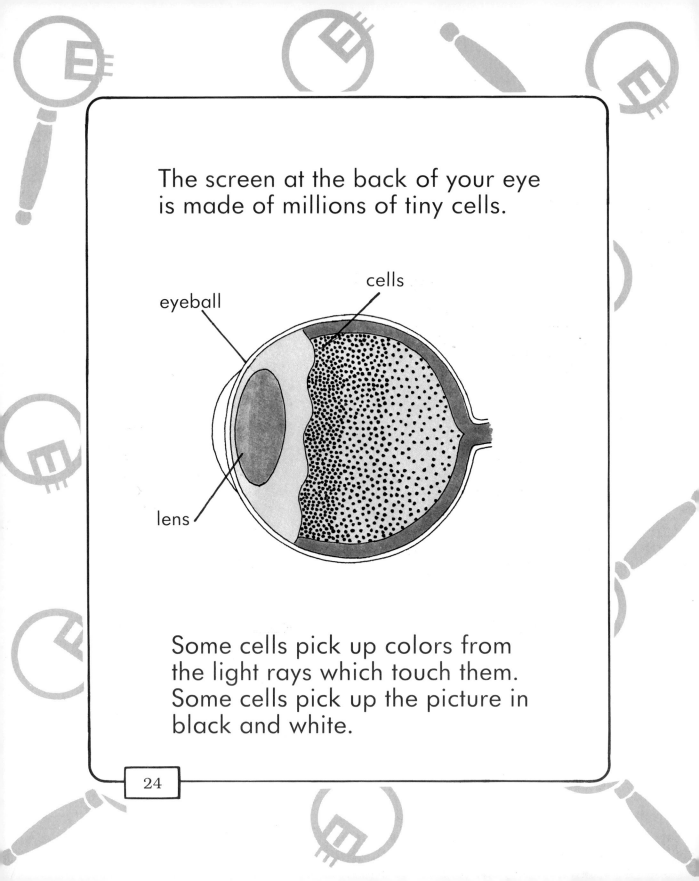

cells

eyeball

lens

Some cells pick up colors from
the light rays which touch them.
Some cells pick up the picture in
black and white.

The color cells in your eyes
need a lot of light
to make them work.
The black and white cells
need less light.

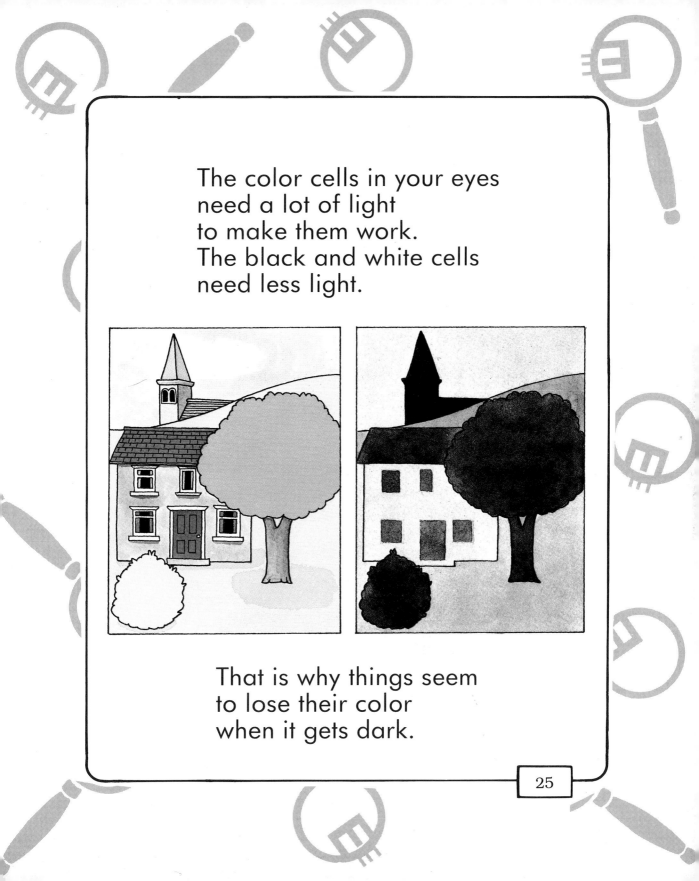

That is why things seem
to lose their color
when it gets dark.

Thin threads called nerves run from the cells at the back of your eyes. They join up into a big nerve which carries the picture from your eye to your brain.

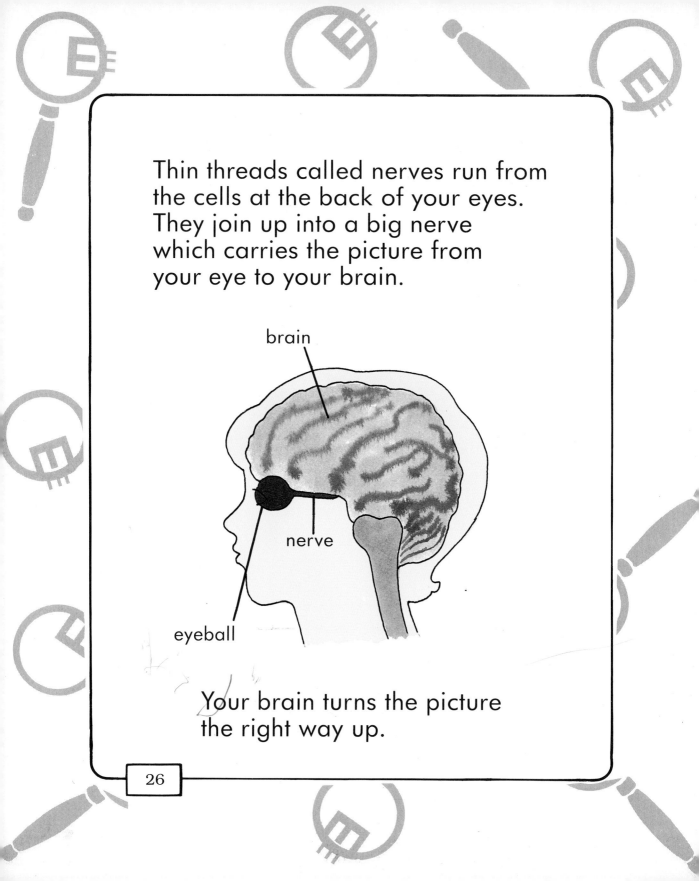

brain

nerve

eyeball

Your brain turns the picture the right way up.

Your brain puts together
pictures from your two eyes.

Close one eye.
Hold out a pencil.
Line it up with the straight edge
of a door or a picture.
Look at the pencil with one eye
and then with the other eye.

Your two eyes make pictures
which are not exactly the same.

Your brain thinks about the pictures that come from your eyes.
It makes sense of what you see.
It tells you what to look at next.

Seeing is something you may do without thinking.
But your eyes and your brain take their jobs quite seriously!

How Does That Happen?

Did you find all these things to do in *What Happens When You LOOK?* If not, turn back to the pages listed here and have some fun seeing how your body works.

1. See how you can get around without seeing. (page 7)
2. See how your head protects your eyes. (page 8)
3. Stare at something without blinking. (page 10)
4. How far around can you see? (page 13)
5. Watch your pupils change size. (page 15)
6. Look at your finger through a magnifying glass. (page 18)
7. See how your eyes focus. (page 20)
8. Watch how your eyes move when you look at things close or far away. (page 21)
9. Make an eye with paper and straws. (page 23)
10. See how your eyes work separately. (page 27)

More Books About Looking and Seeing

Listed below are more books about what happens when you look. If you are interested in them, check your library or bookstore.

The Eye and Seeing. Ward (Franklin Watts)
From Head to Toes: How Your Body Works. Packard (Simon & Schuster)
Look at Your Eyes. Showers (Crowell)
The Magic of Color. Simon (Lothrop, Lee & Shepard)
My Mother Is Blind. Reuter (Childrens Press)
Patrick, Yes You Can. Frevert (Creative Education)
Seeing Is Not Believing. Brandreth (Sterling)
Your Eyes. Adler (Harper & Row)

Where to Find More About Looking and Seeing

Here are some people you can write away to for more information about what happens when you look. Be sure to tell them exactly what you want to know about. Include your full name and address so they can write back to you.

American Foundation for the Blind
15 West 16th Street
New York, New York 10011

International Association of Lions Clubs
300 22nd Street
Oak Brook, Illinois 60570

National Society for the Prevention of Blindness, Inc.
79 Madison Avenue
New York, New York 10016

Public Affairs Pamphlets
381 Park Avenue South
New York, New York 10016

Index